FAITH
MEANS
WAR

Dr. Larry E Adams

WESTBOW
PRESS®
A DIVISION OF THOMAS NELSON
& ZONDERVAN

WestBow Press books may be ordered through
booksellers or by contacting:

WestBow Press
A Division of Thomas Nelson & Zondervan
1663 Liberty Drive
Bloomington, IN 47403
www.westbowpress.com
1 (866) 928-1240

Scripture taken from the King James Version of the Bible.

ISBN: 978-1-9736-9641-4 (sc)
ISBN: 978-1-9736-9640-7 (e)

Print information available on the last page.

WestBow Press rev. date: 08/04/2020

DEDICATION

I write this book to the Church of Jesus Christ. All those whos doors stand ajar in His name and for the love of the Spirit of God. Realizing that He is worthy of all possible honor, confidence and love to the glory of God the Father. We give Him praise.

CONTENTS

FOREWORD

It is clearly understood that the war in heaven was not to be a sign, because the presence of Satan in heaven was a reality. (Ephesians 6:10-12) However, that war ended with Satan and his followers being cast out from the immediate presence of God to the second heaven. And even though there is really only one war against sin and the evil forces of Satan, there are many battles to be fought. And according to the Genesis account of the fall of man, the first institution established by God after creation was the family and it was the focus of attack by Satan.

When man fail from his holy and happy state of being because of his voluntary transgression, sin and death entered all creation. The battlefield of spiritual warfare was established. Understand that we are not warring against flesh and blood according to the scripture, but against principalities and powers and rulers of darkness in high places. (Ephesians 6:12) You could not imagine that in the first dispensation if innocence (Genesis 1:28); just as there was no doubt, worry or fear, there was also no need for faith apart from the fact that man knew God and there was no need for him to hope or wonder about His existence. God walked and talked with man in the garden and they did have a relationship. It was not until the fall of man that sin entered bringing with it doubt, fear, worry, and last but not least a reason to need faith. While faith seems to refer to belief or the act of believing, at one time there was only truth or knowledge. Man did not know like God knew but he knew and trusted God. Man had only the will to obey God. It was not until God's provision of sacrifice and promise that Adam began to exercise faith. God specifically told them that "in the day that thou eatest thereof thou shall surely die". (Gen.2:17) This would mean a separation from God spiritually and in time death. But being the merciful God He is he gave them a promise (Genesis 3: 15-16) that Eve would bear children and live continually. As a result of this promise, Adam named his wife Eve: because she was the mother of all living. Adam perceived the things implied in the promise as a sign of victory over the Devil. And because of the way God revealed His plan to Adam, Adam believed God and His plan of salvation in His promise. We must realize that at this point it could only be by faith that his redemption will occur. Man must depend on faith in God's plan of salvation. But let us not forget the opposition of Satanic forces that would attempt to destroy or prevent any form of faith or righteousness in the world.

For the scriptures say that all that would live Godly shall suffer persecution. (II Timothy 3:12) In all actuality this means war. Therefore we must put on the whole armor of God, that we may be able to stand against the wiles of the Devil (Ephesians 6:16). And above all, taking the shield of faith, with which ye shall be able to quench all the fiery darts of the wicked (Ephesians 6:16). Faith puts God between you and the enemy. "FAITH MEANS WAR". And no man that warreth entagleth himself with the affairs of this life that he may please him who hath chosen him to be a soldier. (II Timothy. 2:4).

As a Christian it is our desire to dwell in peace. Our perception of peace has changed continually from our conversion. Because we have put so much emphasis on the changing of our lives to live in peace we are often unaware that the conversion was not just about how we change but where we change. In other words, The conversion was from the physical realm to the spiritual realm. Our faith has lead us into the realm of spirituality. This means that our understanding and perception of peace takes on a different reality. A reality that is not based on what we understand and can see but faith and trust in God. In this spiritual realm we realize that our real enemy is not within the flesh and blood and of the physical realm but in the spiritual darkness of this world.

(Ephesians 6:12) We cannot see or understand the wickedness in high places therefore we have to rely on Jesus. This is what spiritual warfare is all about. One advantage we have is knowing that Satan desires to keep us in spiritual darkness so that we cannot see his works of wickedness. Lies and deception, lack of faith and trust in God as well as disobedience keeps us in the realm of spiritual darkness. Satan does not want us to see Jesus for who He is, "The light of the world". The moment that you say that you believe you become a part of that light, And the enemy want to put that light out!

INTRODUCTION

As Christians you have entered the spiritual realm and now must depend on faith and put on the whole armor of God. You have entered spiritual warfare and you will fight many battles only to learn that the battles are not yours they are the Lords. Everything in this world has to do with spirituality but God is in control no matter how it looks. As good soldiers we are to stay on the battlefield at all times. Standing on the foundation of truth and with God's approval. And be ready to carry on with the Gospel of peace with God. And with faith, be able to overcome the attacks of the wicked with the word of God. Be ye faithful until death (Revelation 2:10)

Christians often wonder why we are having so many trials and tribulations in so many ways even in areas unexpected. We often forget that we are in very real spiritual warfare and it is not going to stop until God addresses the situation according to His plan. Until that time we are always at war and Satan wants us "dead" not troubled. Considering the circumstances you would think that we would be preparing instead of thinking that we are ever completely prepared for this battle. This poses a problem not knowing that there is never a time of peace outside of the word of God. The reality of being in spiritual warfare is difficult for most Christians to accept as a reality. FAITH MEANS WAR!

ACKNOWLEDGEMENT

I give God all praise and glory for allowing me one more opportunity to share His blessing upon me of being able to exercise his gift of the Word. I thank God and my Lord and Savior Jesus Christ for his gift and opportunity to share with my brothers and sisters in Christ. My primary thanks goes to my Church family and my Pastor, Landis Fisher, who is a dynamic teacher of the Gospel.

I also want to express my deepest gratitude to my wonderful wife Julia who has demonstrated such love and trust that is beyond measure. Together with Jesus we have found happiness and success in simple obedience of the word of God.

THE ABRAHAMIC REVIEW OF FAITH

God had commanded Abraham to separate himself from his father's house and kindred. (Gen 12:1) (II Cor 6:17-18) God's purpose starts with separation from the world. And Scripture teaches us that obedience is better that sacrifice. (I Sam 15:22) Abraham was the father of the faithful and the example of a special relationship with the Father. As a result of that relationship we who are believers are blessed who trust in God. Abraham discovered many spiritual truth concerning faith and fellowship with God that had a profound impact on our lives. (Isa 6:25) Even though God had commanded Abraham, as with us, choice is always there reminding us to stay under the will of God. We learn from Abraham that many times we try to see too much of our faith. But God can be depended on to act the way He has always acted before, He does not change. Being steadfast is important when waiting up under God's will and trusting Him. God gave Abraham a covenant not a compromise!

We Learned through Abraham's experiences that there is a continuing conflict between law and grace. This is as Paul calls it an allegory between the flesh and the Spirit. (Galatians 4:22-31) Abraham was our exemplary model of faith. (Gen 5:6) We learned that salvation does not come through works but by grace through faith in Christ. (Eph 2:8-9) To live in righteousness is to live by faith. And even though Abraham had compromised with his wife he had yet to learn that we must "through faith and patient inherit the promise". (Heb 6:12, 10:35, 36, James 1:3,4, Romans 5:3) Even though Sarah was a godly woman who fell into unbelief the Lord assured her that she would have innumerable descendants through her unborn son who will be called "Ishmael" (God hears). (Gen 16:10-14) Although not the child of the promise but was Abraham's seed. By this we can clearly see the effect that compromising has on our faith to be obedient or have a choice. Christians should never compromise the word of God. (Matt 6:24) It is a disaster to compromise righteousness and there are always consequences. Abraham learned that we should never allow a period of waiting upon the Lord to result in unbelief because it will never bring about God's blessings.

God established an everlasting covenant with Abraham even though he did not realize that meant that the covenant was already fulfilled in the future. Abraham was not promised that he would see that result during his time. When It comes to the father of faith (Abraham), so many lessons must be considered that will strengthen us in our faith.

The fact that God gave Abraham a covenant not a compromise, a promise not a possibility.

(Romans 4:17) Some of the most powerful examples of exemplary faith has been shared by Abraham's experiences. Nothing can alter God's plans or His promises. (Isa 55:11) Doubt comes through the door of your will.

The experiences of Abraham consisted basically of four great crises in the lost and surrender of things that He loved the most. His country and his kindred, his plans for Ishmael his son, his nephew Lot who also was a believer and Isaac, his son, "thine only son" who he loved. God tested Abraham's sincerity, loyalty and faith as He will do the same with us. (James 1:2,12-14) (I Pet 1 6-7) As children of the faith our faith, as Abraham's must go far beyond understanding, perception and will be led by obedience, sincerity and loyalty. (I Sam 15:22) (Romans 12:1) Make sure that we don't love God's promise more than we do God. Abraham's son could not mean more to him than God. God will allow us to be tested in order to strengthen our faith in Him.

We could do well to study carefully the principles guiding the preparations for marriage relationships offered in the choosing of a bride for Isaac. Considering how important it is and never taking for granted. (Proverb 18:22) (Proverb 19:14) A prudent wife is from the Lord and is not lost that she should be found. But it is clear that this relationship depends on your relationship in the Lord at that time. We should agree that choosing a wife involves three persons rather than two. Sometimes it may seem like a long time that God would answer our prayers but (Isa 65:24) says that it is already done. The principles that must be learned as taught in scriptures is 1. Ask God to send good seed. In other words ask God for a mate. 2. Make sure you are under God's will. 3 Pray that your choice will be God's choice according to His word. 4. Don't be deceived by what you see and what others say. 5. Know that when God sends you someone don't try to match them with your exceptions. For God is Good and knows every heart.

PUT ON THE WHOLE ARMOR OF GOD (EPHESIANS 6:13)

We all may not perceive that we are at war and have been since the fall of man. Those of us who recognize this fact realize that preparation is necessary. Regardless of age or occupation God is no respecter of persons. Whether we are able to perceive or understand why we are at war is not a question but a warning. We must realize that we must study war for the rest of our lives because the prince of the power of the air is a spirit that now works in the sons of disobedience (Ephesians 2:2). Nevertheless, those of us who are Christians would recall that scripture says that the dragon, which is Satan was angry with the woman (Church,believers) and went to make war with the remnant of her seed, who keep the commandments of God, and have the testimony of Jesus Christ. (Rev 12:17) It has been made clear to us that we are in spiritual warfare and that within ourselves. Therefore, our weapons of warfare are not carnal but mighty through God to the pulling down of strongholds, casting down reasoning, and every high thing that stands against the knowledge of God. (II Corinthian 10:4-6) The best preparation we can have is staying in the word of God (Armor).

The most common concern in any warfare is what kind of protection will we use or armor will we ware. We want to make sure that we are covered in every area of our exposure. We are trusting that the "whole" armor of God is assured. No partiality of any kind is acceptable. Putting on the whole armor of God takes time, patience, knowledge and perseverance. It must be put on the right way, with the Gospel of peace and the shield of faith. (Ephesians 6:13-16) We are reminded that the word of God is sharper than any two edge sword, piercing even to the dividing asunder of soul and spirit, and is a discerner of thought and intents of the heart. (Hebrew 4:12)

It is important that we keep in touch with our general which is God the Father and Jesus to receive our instructions on a daily basis through his word. And never ceasing to pray always along with being reminded what Jesus has promised us that He would be with us always. Prayer is the most powerful opportunity we have along with living and trusting in His promise. We must according to the scripture "earnestly contend for the faith which was once delivered unto the saints". (Jude 3) because there are ungodly men who crept in unawares, who were of old ordained to this condemnation, turning the grace of our God into lasciviousness, and denying the only Lord God, and our Lord Jesus Christ." And the angels who kept not their first estate, but left their own habitation, he hath reserved in everlasting chains under darkness unto the judgment of the great day." (Jude 6)

No man that warreth entangleth himself with the affairs of this life, that he may please him who hath chosen him to be a soldier.

2 Timothy 2:4

SPIRITUAL WARFARE REVEALED

A question was asked of King Ahab who had forsaken the commandments of God, "How long halt ye between two opinions?" This question was reminiscent of Joshua's challenge, "choose you this day whom ye will serve" (Joshua 24:15). Baalism would accommodate other gods, but Jehovah demanded total and uncompromising loyalty and worship from an individual. For all practical purposes, an invitation was given by Elijah to Ahab and the eight hundred fifty prophets of Baal to prove themselves publicly their ability to have power over Jehovah. The agreement was that the decided advantage would go to the deity that responded in sending fire upon a slaughtered bullock and would be unequivocally declared the true God. Only Elijah had stood alone as God's spokesman because the hundred prophets had been hidden away by Obadiah and were inactive. (I Kings 3:16) The prophets of Baal had failed in their attempt to get a response even to the point of sacrificing themselves. In response to Elijah's request for Jehovah to show Himself to be God, "the fire of the Lord fell and consumed to the whole altar. The result of this demonstration of divine visitation was so overwhelming that the people responded," The Lord, he is the God:; The Lord, he is the God" (I Kings 18:39). An excellent example of faith on Elijah's part allowed spiritual warfare to be exposed to the people of Israel that they might see the power of God and know that there is only one true and living God. FAITH MEANS WAR! But even after this great display of faith, it wasn't long afterwards that Jezebel promptly responded with her intent to kill Elijah the prophet (I King 19:1). Elijah was found running for his life at a time when prospects for a nationwide spiritual revival was possible. He had spoiled them by abandoning in discouragement while fleeing for his life and leaving. FAITH MEANS WAR?

After Elijah had fled to the wilderness of Paran, he had hid himself under a juniper tree in deep depression and was requesting death. Thinking that he was the last of the prophets, God rebuked him to even consider that this war was over. He was strengthened by a heavenly messenger and despite the fact that Elijah had failed in keeping his faith at such a critical time, God had showed His own true and innermost essence of grace, by rescuing, preserving, and restoring his people by remaining faithful and gracious as He promised.

FAITH MEANS WAR and God can always be depended on to act the way he has always acted in the past. In the conflict between holy and unholy angels, (Dan 10:21) It was revealed to Daniel that the reason for the delay in the answer of his prayer was because the prince of the kingdom of Persia had detained the messenger of the Lord. The messenger was detained for twenty-one days because of this spiritual warfare…It wasn't until Michael the Archangel came to help the messenger that he was able to deliver the answer requested. No doubt the messenger was detained by supernatural beings mainly principalities and powers. Likewise, the prince of Persia must have been one of Satan's demons. What a spiritual warfare it must have been that a messenger of God could be held off for twenty-one days from answering Daniel's prayer. Obviously what was contained in the message was of great interest to the opposing forces because it carried a prophecy of "what shall befall thy people in the latter days". Daniel was about to receive a revelation that was outside of his understanding. It had been revealed to him that there was spiritual warfare in the air that we on earth knew very little about. Daniel had been overwhelmed to the point where he was too weak to receive the revelation and had to be strengthen by the messenger. FAITH MEANS WAR even if we have no knowledge or understanding to receive the truth of it. Michael was known as the war angel or one of the chief princes (10:13) who came to help the messenger. He was also the prince of Israel to protect and fight her battles (10:21). In conclusion of this revelation, the prophecy of Israel's future to the Maccabees and beyond has been given this message and in scripture (Dan 11:45)

Paul states that because we are spirit filled believer in Christ, "we wrestle not against flesh and blood, but against principalities, against powers, against the rulers of darkness of this world, against the spiritual wickedness in high places (Eph 6:12). This means that we are in the midst of spiritual warfare and must arm ourselves. However, the weapons of warfare are not carnal, but almighty through God to the pulling down of strongholds (II Cor 10:4) According to Paul in the scriptures, we are to cast down imaginations and every high thing that exalteth itself against the knowledge of God, and bring into captivity every thought to the obedience of Christ. We must" put on the whole armor of God, that ye may be able to stand against the wiles of the devil "(Eph 6:11).

On Paul's first missionary journey through the isle of Paphos, he encountered a certain sorcerer, a false prophet, a Jew, whose name was Bar-Jesus (Acts 13:6). Satan tried to resist him by seeking to turn away the Roman proconsul from the faith but was struck blind by the hand of the Lord as Paul withstood him. As a result of this display of power of these servants of the Lord over his magician adviser, the proconsul believed the doctrine of the Lord (Acts 13:12). Paul described this Magos (Greek) as "full of all deceit and all mischief, thou son of devil, enemy of all righteousness. Paul's journey began with a direct confrontation with Satan who knew what Paul's mission was to the rest of the world. Satan was not able to resist because the weapon that Paul used was "behold, the hand of the Lord. FAITH MEANS WAR and any resistance to the faith means war. Faith is the overcoming principle in the world conflict. "For whatever is born of God overcometh the world, even our faith" (John 5:4).

FAITH MEANS WAR and there is something to guard against in the spiritual warfare. In each stage of the believer's life within, wages a constant war against any resistance to its growth. During the physical stage the war is against sins and the natural life. On the spiritual level the war is against the supernatural enemy. When Christians find themselves being attacked by evil spirits it is because they are spiritual and they are now within the spiritual realm. This spiritual warfare would rarely ever happen to unbelievers. If you are truly a believing Christian, there is no chance of your soul being lost but continuous conflict with the flesh and its danger. Prayer and faith are the only weapons of warfare we have. We must however, be able to distinguish between the natural and supernatural disturbances. We must try to exercise daily the will to deny any opposition to our purpose for being. Also, focus on the spirit and guard against spiritual influence by the wicked.

As soldiers we are supposed to be led by the Holy Spirit. One thing that seems to keep us from cooperating with the Holy Spirit is our lack of patience to wait during time of battle or spiritual conflict. We seem to have problems relating to the personality of the Holy Spirit. There is a difference in the way the Holy Spirit and the evil spirit works in our lives. The Holy Spirit inspires people to willingly respond to a work acceptable to God while an evil spirit attempts to take over the will totally and replace that will with that which is not acceptable to God or is against His will. This fundamental difference stands between the works of the Holy Spirit and that of an evil spirit. In spiritual warfare, we must attack Satan without end. We ought to have a combat attitude as soldiers but in the Spirit of God, praying to defeat the wiles of the devil and all his works. What has been misunderstood is the fact that the spiritual life is a life daily fighting. To move warfare from a spiritual life is to render it unspiritual. This life is a life of suffering, laboring, watching, and waiting. We are constantly burdened by weariness and trials. A total disregard for one's personal happiness and a life apart from the Father.

The world today does not believe in a literal devil, it simply refers to this as meaning an evil principle from without. However, the Bible teaches an evil personality. There are several names that refer to the Devil-"a great dragon", "that old serpent," "Satan," and "the accuser of the brethren". All of these names actually describe his works and personality.

It is believed by Bible scholars that there will be a series of battles fought in the middle of the Tribulation Period and Satan will fight vigorously with Michael and the heavenly hosts immediately after the rapture of the Church. At this time, the Tribulation period will not only be a time of war but unseen by men. You could imagine the atmosphere around the cross as Jesus was crucified. No doubt there were the most conflicting spiritual forces ever imagined. Even the resurrection on the third day resulted in a devastating blow to Satan and his demons. But during the Tribulation Period, Michael will cast Satan and his angels down to earth. Satan will no longer have access to the throne of God day and night accusing the brethren. Satan's angels will no longer be known as the principalities and powers of the air" because they will be limited to the earth (Revelation 12:12). And after Satan's final anti-Semitic crusade, "pit time" for Satan and his host "Hallelujah"! Praise the Lord!

TRIALS AND TRIBULATIONS

Jesus says, "in this world ye shall have tribulation", (John 16:33). This is to be interpreted not just that we are going to have trouble in life but because of our faith we will be tested in trials and afflictions. (James 1:1-2, II Cor 8:2) In spiritual warfare we are on a battlefield of faith. It is not a matter of who is the strongest but who will stand. Because he Lord says "not by might nor by power but by my Spirit saith the Lord. (Zechariah 4:6b) We are to learn that faith will overcome in this battle. Since this spiritual warfare is also a battle of the mind, decision making, trust and knowledge, we must constantly stand on the word of God.

Trials and tribulations does not necessarily mean suffering and pain. It could be a test of our perception of the principles of life. Part of our learning about the principles of life can be taught by the things that we suffer. (Hebrew 5:8) We have learned that all things work for our good because we love God. (Romans 8:28) We should not forget that we are passing through a sin cursed world and enemy territory where there will be continuous battles of all kinds. Our General, which is our Lord and Savior Jesus Christ has never told that it would be easy but did say He would be with us even until the end of the world. (Matthew 28:20)

A perfect example of the presence of spiritual warfare on a personal basis is stated by Paul "He says that "he delights in the law of God after the inward man; but I see another law in my members, warring against the law of my mind, and bringing me into captivity to the law of sin which is in my members. He cries "O wrecked man that I am! Who shall deliver me from this body of death? (Romans 7: 22-24) The answer to this question is the law of the Spirit of life in Christ Jesus will free us from the law of sin and death. While keeping in mind that we are soldiers on this battlefield and that no man having put his hands to the plough and looking back is fit for the kingdom of God. (Luke 9:62) We must be faithful because no man that warreth entagleth himself with the affairs of this life, that he may please Him who has chosen him to be a soldier. (II Timothy 2:3-4)

Putting on the whole armor of God also means that we must be aware of the cunning craftiness of men be of which they lie in wait to deceive even with our own perception. We must always remember that faith means war and that's at all times in every way as long as we live. Our awareness must be in the word of the Lord at all times as we should always pray. The moment you step into the spiritual realm (or become a believer) through faith it will take that same faith in our Lord and Savior Jesus Christ to bring you through this battle. Notice the scripture does not tell us to fight but withstand. The fight in the spiritual realm is not a physical one but a spiritual one. Thinking that we can fight this battle physically is a bad perception and you give victory to the enemy. This is a spiritual battle and it will be won spiritually. Just be still and stand on faith and God will fight your battle.

THE REALITY
OF FAITH

In Hebrew, the terms for faith simply means "firmness" of "stability" of the trust that one person has in another person. In the Greek New Testament, the relationship of faith is focused upon God. In reality, the extent of the word is to mean "to trust", have confidence in, and correct perception of. The scriptures define faith as being the substance of things hoped for and the evidence of things not seen. (Hebrew 1:1) Faith reminds us of the fact that God is the cause and reason of the existence of things and is according to his purpose. For without faith it is impossible to please God.

Faith is a person's way of moving into the spiritual realm of life and is not always religious in its content and context. Since the beginning of mankind, we have always searched for something that makes us feel worthy for existing. Our universal concern has always perceived the issue of faith. We require meaning in our lives. We need purpose as well as priorities in order to get some grasps on the big picture.

Christians believe that Jesus Christ is God's revelation, and faith is needed to perceive and understand its meaning. In religious experience, to believe is to perceive. Our beliefs are derived from perceptions of life's events. Since our perception of life's event it has a profound effect on our ethical way of living. When divine revelation takes the place in the lives of men, they experience change in their perceptions of themselves, the world, and of reality. They become new creatures.

"Faith, like perception is subjective, personal and direct. Faith is supernatural, not irrational. Reducing religious experience to mere philosophical argument misses the point and overlooks the purpose of religious faith." [1]

Faith as an act of surrender involves the surrender of an acute sense of total responsibility for everything other people do. We sometimes feel that we are a failure unless we can be everything and totally succeed persons in our care. When parents accept total responsibility for the thought, values and acts of their children, this is not the giving up of one's need to be totally responsible and all powerful but is an everyday exercise of faith. Any other kind of faith would be nothing but a sort of substitute that would become a liable insulation in our lives.

When the act of surrender is seen as a demonstration of faith, it can have a psychosomatic dimension. When a person feels that they must be totally responsible, the physiology of the body is subject to the unnecessary stress. The Spirit of God must

[1] James W. Fowler 1940-Harper & Row, Publishers, San Francisco Cambridge, Hagerstown, New York, Phildelphia, London, Mexico City 1817

influence any personal gains from family support of friends to avoid adopting a sinful way of life. A total surrender to faith will find understanding.

A total surrender of faith will realize that Jesus must not only be accepted as our Savior but also as our Lord. This is the meaning of total surrender in reference to total understanding. As we struggle to maintain a life of faith we find ourselves wrestling with the understanding of Lordship of our lives. We forget that the power of faith does not come by us but through us from God. We are not only responsible but accountable for acceptable service to God in exercising the power of faith. (Heb 11:6) The power of faith can very well be measured by the degree of lordship in our lives. If Jesus is totally accepted in our lives as Lord and Savior, then the power of faith will be pleasing to God and will be our reasonable service. If we are going to overcome we must learn to live and use the kind of faith that it takes to be victorious. Since we don't know from a daily basis what we have to overcome, we need to make sure that our relationship with God is one that will supply us with a faith that will overcome whatever obstacle that stands opposed to us. Our decision; to overcome will always be influenced by the quality of lordship, relationship, and stewardship in our lives.

No Man, having put his hand to the plough and looking back, is fit for the Kingdom of God

Luke 9:62

THE TEST OF FAITH

After the first dispensation of the fall of man from his start of innocence for which he was created, he now stands on the threshold of entering spiritual battlefields of tests. During these periods of time of his obedience to some specific revelation of the will of God, he will begin to exercise and flex the muscles of his faith by use of his conscience and moral responsibility. This presents the second era of dispensation after receiving the first promise of redemption (Gen 4:1-8,14). Man's sin was a rebellious act against a specific command of God (Gen 2:16-17) and marked a transitional period experiencing theoretical knowledge of good and evil (3:5-7:22). He has now found himself entering the realm of moral experience in the wrong way or a way that was not intended by God. As a result of this sinful approach, man became as God through personal experience of the difference between good and evil, but in the wrong way. Though he was placed by God under the stewardship of moral responsibility. He was expected to be accountable to all known good and obtain from all known evil. Also, as a representative of the finish work of Christ. A blood sacrifice was required in to redeem man.1

The Noahic Covenant subjected humanity to a new test of the faith that was handed down to this new generation. Although man continued to be morally responsible to God as in ("Render unto God the things that are God's," Matt, 22:21), God delegated to him specific areas of His authority of which he was to obey God through submission to his fellow man (Render therefore unto Caesar the things which are Caesar's" Matt 22:21). By this, God instituted a corporate relationship of man to man in human government. All powers are ordain of God. And to resist the power is to resist God. In the preceding generation restraint upon men was internal (Gen 6:3) because God's spirit was working through moral responsibility. Now we have the power of civil government a new external restraint. The Noahic Covenant reaffirms the conditions of the life of man, having fallen and institutes the principle of human government to curb the outbreak of sin.

FAITH MEANS WAR and according to I Corinthians 3:13, every man's work shall be tested or manifested for the day shall declare it, because it shall be revealed by fire: and the fire shall test every man's work of what sort it is. Therefore, even though we are expected to study to show ourselves approved unto God a workman that need not to be ashamed, rightly dividing the word of truth. (II Timothy 2:15) As a soldier of Christ we are to fight the good fight of faith, lay hold on eternal life, unto which thou art also called and hast professed a good profession before many witnesses. (1 Timothy 6:12) And if you have faith in God in enemy territory remember you are also an enemy and that means war.

Sometimes we welcome the test of faith as in Elijah's confrontation with the four hundred prophets of Baal. His demonstration of faith reveals a specific relationship with God the father trusting his response on request to establish the truth of who the God of Israel is. But even though the God of Israel granted his request the next episode he found himself running for his life. His perception of the situation was altered by fear and he found himself running for his life. He realized that he did not take the stand that he was worthy of, trusting God. Nevertheless, we face the same issues many times. We must remember that God deals with us personally according to our measure of faith (Romans 12:3) that we may grow by testing. Faith waivers that's why all our strength comes from the Lord. (Psalms 73:26)

"War a good warfare"

1 Timothy 1:18

THE POWER OF FAITH

Spiritual warfare is a realm that is beyond our control. And since we have been made aware of the fact that we must arm ourselves, it would only make sense that we should know what kind of power we have to defend ourselves against. Taking in consideration the Greek New Testament definition of the word "power", we would be surprised to find that its usage is not always clearly understood. For instance, there are basically two possible meanings for the same word depending upon how it is used. Many times, in scripture, the word "Power" is not meaning a source or possession but rather a position to receive from a source, such as authority. Take for example, Matthew 9:8 says," who had given such power (authority) unto men". This refers

DR. LARRY E ADAMS

to political rather than spiritual power. But in
Acts 1:8, it states, "but ye shall receive power,
after that the Holy Ghost is come upon you."
This reference to power is spiritual rather than
political. However, this power was not given
to man but as the result of the presence of
the Holy Spirit there was power (spiritual)
working through men for God's purpose.
God never gave men power but authority. But
men received the Holy Spirit as the result of
them giving themselves to God to be used
for His purpose. Power works through men
for God not for men through God. Jesus says
that all power is given to Him in heaven and
in earth. (Matthew 28:18) God did not give
man power he gave them authority. There is
a big difference between having power and
having authority. When men think of having
power, they think of the possession of it rather
than a supplied source. Having authority, on
the other hand, puts man in a position to use
power as a source to accomplish the task. The
problem is, men don't want authority, they
want power. Authority leaves God in control

but power puts man in control. Authority is taking a position to use obedience and faith in depending on God. Power is taking control and depending on you.

God didn't give man control, He gave them authority go let Him control. All power and control is in God's hands. But be careful of the fact that since men were created in the image and likeness of God, you will be attracted by power. Actually, it was given to men to desire authority not power. It wasn't until sin entered the hearts of men that man separated himself from God thereby desiring to have power over his own life.

Authority gives power the opportunity to favor the position. The worse thing that could happen to man is when he comes into the mentality of having power and control, and Satan knows it. We can't even imagine what real power is like. Therefore, what makes us think that we can possess it. First of all, when you come into the mentality of having power, you automatically lose your position of authority from God. You also begin to believe that you don't need God, you are in control. But don't forget, there are also other things that go along with the attribute of having power. For instance, you need to know everything and be every place at one time. If not, you are not in control. You need to understand how, when and where to apply your power, and your perception must be beyond human.

So, if you have power, then there is no need for authority. That would only put you under someone else's control. Men who have power don't take orders, they give them. You will be surprised of the high; minded and pride that develops in a man's heart when he believes he has power. You can't show or tell him anything, he stands alone. As a matter of fact, you can no longer call him man because he has made himself God. Men struggle through life trying to control and get power over everything, even their own lives. They feel that this is necessary in order to survive or accomplish our goals in life. But life is not about power, it is about spirit. (John 6:63)

It is high time that men stop using mentality of having power as a source for living their life. Men don't need power, men need God. Let's put ourselves back under the authority of God. The benefits are remarkable and the job will get done. (Matthew 6:33) Men have a war to fight and a responsibility to render. This area of concern in our lives is another spiritual battlefield. If you want healing, take a position of authority to be healed, there is power in that! If you want your families to fall in line, take a position of authority from God there is power in that! If you think you have power, give it up for authority from God, there is power in that! You know why things are not right at home or on the job? Because men will not take authority from God. Don't you know that people will know who you are and who gave you the authority to act the way you do? The Lord says if I be lifted up I will draw all men under me. (John 12:32) In other words if a man doesn't stand with authority from God, he will fall for power.

There is no discharge in that war, neither shall wickedness deliver those that are given to it.

Ecclesiastes 8:8

"THE BATTLE OF THE MIND"

There are six different Hebrew words that are translated "mind" and some of these ancient words become "heart", "soul", and "attitude" when translated to English.[2]

Sometimes the word can even be referred to mean "determination" (as in Nehemiah 4:6 where it reads that people" had a mind to work")[3]. New Testament writers would refer to the mind as a fleshy mind, vain mind, corrupt

---

[2] D.M. Lake, "Mind," in The Zoudervan Pictoral Encyclopedia of the Bible, vol.4, ed. Merrill C. Tenney (Grand Rapids: Zoudervan, 1975), 228-9

[3] This quotation from Nehemia is taken from the King James version of the Bible (KJV) which uses the words "mind to work". The NIV says "the people worked with all their hearts."

mind, evil mind, blinded mind, wicked mind, reprobate mind, or doubtful mind? Believe it or not we as Christians do have in us a presence of the mind of Christ.[4]

By altering the attitude of our mind, we can ultimately change the quality of our lives which is closely related to how we think. The Bible teaches that we are trichotomous beings composed of three parts as body, spirit (supernatural nature) and soul (the emotions, will, and mind). (1 Thess 5:23) The Bible has a "tripartite" view of human beings and portrays not only a struggle with our mental inclination and our actions but with our spirit and our flesh. For example, the strife of the two natures spoken by Paul in scripture. (Rom 7:15-24) We can imagine the powerful influence the mind has to confront especially in the midst of spiritual warfare.

First of all, in order to be mentally alert and prepared, scripture teaches us to "gird up the loins of your mind". (1 Peter 1:13) They were not only to expect an attack physically

[4] I Corinthians 2:16, TLB

and spiritually but mentally as well. The battlefield would be of the mind. Peter was telling the people that they must be ready for a hostile world of persecution and that believers were to avoid fear and discouragement but be strong and composed. Have a sober spirit that is self-assured. (1Peter 1:10-14) We should be spiritually self-controlled and spiritually hopeful at all times. Bible teaches that we should be "transformed by the renewing of your mind." (Rom 12:2) Paul explains how this is to take place with instructions that focus on the physical body being brought into subjection fist as a link to a renewed mind. The renewing of your mind is not focused on the body but the disciplined living that the person does that would favor Gods will by sacrificing that way of honoring Him. As a result of this change they are more likely to be characterized by a graceful and righteous life. Through willful determination our change of attitude will make a difference in how we live.

Of course, this will make a difference in how we think. Most important the results will help us to establish a much-needed relationship with our Heavenly Father. At this point we should keep our minds open and allow God to renew our minds and our footsteps. The battle of the mind starts with us and our faith that we have in Jesus. Our minds and our perceptions are constantly being attacked by Satan on a daily basis. This is why we need the renewing of our mind.

In the renewing of our minds we must be mentally alert, spiritually self-controlled and spiritually hopeful. Though the Bible is telling us to "gird up" our minds, it's talking about the mind that we have as a result of our transformation. For the scriptures teach to "let this mind be in you that was in Christ Jesus". (Phil 2:5) We are to prepare for action spiritually. This instruction was focused at Christians that their minds receive the message with a clear understanding. A careful investigation is expected of a spiritual mind and those who are aware of the intellectual trends around them. We should always be spiritually hopeful despite the fact that there is so much satanic craftiness and influential temptation around us. We should realize that the mind is the main playing field of Satan and the world is his result.

It is believed that mind renewal is linked to how we care for our bodies. (Rom12:1-2) Actually this is focused on the type of spiritual influence and obedience we should have as we share the death, burial, and resurrection demonstrated by our Lord and Savior Jesus Christ. Our bodies are given as a living sacrifice as proof that we have this same mind that our Lord has lead by his Spirit. The Spirit is what renews the mind and we are transformed as the result of that. When we have been transformed, we will have a more realistic self-image, a care for the needs of others and a purpose for living. At the same time, we will build a stronger relationship with God.

So many Psychologists and others who study the mind give so much attention to the negative emotions that they don't really know how these positive feelings come about. The Apostle Paul wrote while in jail to encourage the Philippians about joy, peace, and even freedom from anxiety. He also told them to let their minds think about whatever was true, right, pure, lovely, admirable, excellent, and worthy of praise. Does not this seem somewhat strange that a person would be able to physically change their reality alone with just their minds? These states of mind or attributes could only come through the Spirit of God. These were the fruits of the Spirit. (Ephesians 5:9-12) Paul mentions nothing about feelings but about the gifts of the spirit. For we know that in this spiritual warfare our enemies are the world, the flesh (feelings), and Satan. Let us not forget that even though Paul was in the condition that he was in he was not taking heed to his minds but his spirit and the grace of God. (Romans 7:24-25) The spiritually mature mind avoids unrealistic, extreme thinking, and develops a "spiritual" perspective in all areas of life. Christians recognize that all have sinned and fall short of the Glory of God but know that we can be forgiven if we confess our sins and repent He is faithful and just to cleanse us of our sins and restore us to righteousness. As Christians, we need to understand that there is no such thing as "mental illness" apart from injury, tumors, and other brain problems. By adopting this terminology man is simply blinding a Christian world view that asks the question how could a non-organic entity (whatever it may be cause a non-organic illness?) The body is what gets ill the living organism. Don't be deceived by this medical terminology used to describe a non-medical problem as having an illness.

They chose new gods; then was
war in the gates

Judges 5:8

ENEMY NUMBER ONE "COMPROMISING"

One of the first enemies we will encounter in faithful living is being tempted to compromise. Even though Satan would have you leave that door open in consideration that it might be a pass for peace and reconciliation, it is not according to the word of God. Compromising with the world has disastrous and deceptive consequences to God's people. Beginning with the philosophy of the world asking the question, "does it work?" should not be a reason to perceive compromising as the right way to achieve their purpose. Question should be "is it biblical and practical for faithful living?". Scripture teaches us that there is a way that seems right to a man but the end thereof are the ways of death. (Prov 16:25)

FAITH MEANS WAR and we often time forget that we are in a very real spiritual warfare and things are not always going to be as they seem. Some of Gods greatest servants that are filled with love and compassion can err by allowing themselves to tolerate everything and everyone especially his own family members thus compromising the truth of God. His purpose may be to keep the peace but it won't keep God's word. The world will never see the peace of God that passes all understanding. Faithful living in this spiritual warfare must always depend on biblical standards no matter how it seems or what our perceptions are.

One of the biggest problems we have in this world is relationship. It started with our broken relationship with God the Father. Now we find relationships complicated and difficult to understand. Most don't perceive or understand how to have a relationship or its purpose. The Bible itself is a book of relationships, first with God and then with each other. God's purpose for relationships has always been about "oneness". The same as His purpose for us that we might be one with the Father. (John 17:11) There cannot be a world without relationships. On the other hand, we must realize that in every area of our lives we will experience trials and tough decisions. We can even find ourselves tolerating unnecessary circumstances that require a different type of love. That is, "tough love". A love that comes with the debt but without understanding. (Rom 13:8) Satan will tempt you to the point where you can't see in the flesh what you need to see in the spirit. When it comes to relationships, it is very real spiritual warfare. Satan uses compromising to suck us into wrong relationships. Relationships that should not be natural (*What We Don't Understand About Relationships*, by Dr. Larry Adams) but first spiritual according to the word.

A good example of being pulled into a compromising situation is in the case of Jehoshaphat in scripture. He gave his son in marriage probably to reunite the two kingdoms. He then accepted the hospitality of Ahab and gave his word to go into battle with him. Sometimes when we make decisions even for a good cause it is still compromising. And if you have the Spirit of God in you it will disturb your conscience. Jehoshaphat regretted that he had given his word, especially after a prophet of God had prophesied against Ahab's expedition. He then found himself being naively agreeing and trusting people more so than God. Had it not been for God's grace Jehoshaphat would have been killed. We can learn from the experiences of Jehoshaphat in how and why we should guard against wrong relationships and compromising. Scriptures teaches not to be unequally yoked with unbelievers. (II Cor 6:14) It's amazing how a Christian will sacrifice and rationalize being disobedient even though there will be serious consequences. If you have already made the mistake of marrying an unbeliever scripture tells us to remain married but try to live a godly life. (I Cor 7: 12-16) Even though scripture teaches "bad company corrupts good morals" (I Cor 15:33) don't be deceived to thinking that you need to compromise to form a social relationship. Remember God hates the wicked, so should we. (Ps 5:5) His conscience was reminding him of his responsibility to the Lord. Love for the sake of unity that compromises cardinal truth is not biblical love.

Being truly faithful in this spiritual warfare will require that total commitment to the faith in God's word be trusted as the only way. Because FAITH MEANS WAR we recognize our enemies to be the world, the flesh, and Satan. One thing we learned about this spiritual warfare is that we are never alone. And if we think about it, we are members of the body of Christ and never sin alone. That sin effects the whole body. Likewise, when we compromise isn't that also with the whole body? Be aware. We will never help sinners if we compromise our standards which is God's word. Nothing good has ever come out of compromising. Be a no compromising Christian.

Churches in our day are full of professing Christians who think that it is OK to keep one foot in the world, and enjoy the pleasures of this world. They are saying to themselves "as long as I have Jesus" that makes it OK. The question is, are you sure you have Jesus? Paul tells us that in scriptures to examine ourselves whether we are in the faith: (II Corinthians 13:5) prove yourselves. No compromise is what the Gospel is all about. Scripture also teaches us that we cannot serve two masters either we will hate the one, and love the other: or else he will hold to the one, and despise the other. (Matthew 6:24) you are either for the Lord or against Him.

Have you denied yourselves and totally given your life to Christ? (Luke 9:23) Remember we are to be in the world but not of the world. (John 17:16)

Jesus says we must deny ourselves (Matthew 16:24). Seems to me to mean that we should give up any worldly pleasures that we still try to cling on to. Did not Jesus ask us in the beginning to count the cost of discipleship? (Luke 14:28) God is looking for those who give their all for Him. Just like there is no such thing as a half of a belief certainly there is no half of a heart. There is either all or nothing at all. God is looking for those to worship Him in spirit and truth. No need for compromising there is only one right way and that is Jesus. (John 14:6) There are those who will disagree with you but this is why FAITH MEANS WAR and no man, having put his hand to the plough, and looking back, is fir for the Kingdom of God. (Luke 9:62)

CHRISTIANS TRAPPED IN MATRIMONY

In this age of dispensation that Christianity refers to as the Church age, we are experiencing some devastating attacks on the families of the church. Not to our surprise that some of these attacks are brought upon us by ourselves. The first institution that God created was the family. This relationship was ordained by God. God created relationships for his purpose and the whole idea of a relationship was "oneness". God wanted man to be with him. Scripture teaches us that God created male and female and that the woman was made for the man not the man for the woman and that they were both equal. (I Cor 11:8-9) Even though society has turned its back on God and his teachings and has denied the power of the Holy Spirit God has continued to be merciful and gracious with love everlasting that man might turn from his wicked ways. Realizing that it is the family that makes up the church and Satan is smart enough to know that to destroy the family would be the place to start. Whatever persuasions, compromising, lies, and turning our backs on God would simply open the door to destruction for the family. The bad decisions we make about serving the one who is protecting us is not realized until it is too late.

So many Christians have fallen up under matrimony not realizing what they have committed too. Believe it or not most people don't realize what matrimony and marriage is all about and therefore marry for different reasons including selfish ones. The problem is, we have forgotten that God still gives husbands and wives but because of the stubbornness of our hearts to wait on him we find ourselves allowing our flesh and our perceptions the opportunity to help God out resulting in a persuasive attitude leading to a bad decision. Righteousness and unrighteousness seems to make no difference when it comes to our need or Gods purpose for our lives. God only joins together the righteous, in other words those who have a special relationship with Him spiritually. "What God has joined together let no man take apart! The two have become one forever. If you have made the mistake of marrying an unbeliever, and I say mistake only because I assume that you are familiar with scripture that says "Be ye not unequally yoked with unbelievers for what fellowship hath righteousness with unrighteousness? "(II Cor 6:14) We should consider that God forgives and that He wants to save your marriage not make you miserable.

God has all power in Heaven and in Earth and Jesus has died for our sins and if we believe that we have the authority to fill Gods purpose for our lives. One of the most important things to remember as a believer is that God has all power and that power works but not against our will as a believer. God will not make a person do anything. He never has and never will. This is a vanity belief that God will make a spouse or child do what is right, not so. The only thing that stands in the way of God's power working in your marriage or relationships is your will to let the Holy Spirit do his work. The Bible tells us that the Holy Spirit will either draw you or drive you away. My concern is that Christians have given up on their marriage or have accepted the failure and making excuses for their spouses. They either won't go to Church or respect the church or their spouses. They make up excuses or offer false compromising in exchange for having their way. They even try to make it as difficult as they can to continue having their way. Blaming and throwing your mistakes at you and accusing you of not being the Christian you are trying to be. Not even feeling that they even owe you an explanation of why they should worship with you. For whatever reason they don't fear God or you and your character as a Christian. What they don't realize is that they took a vow with the Lord first and then with each other. That means that your marriage consists of three persons not just two. You, your wife, and Jesus. The Lord has put you together based on your vow. You are either joined in matrimony as one or by law as two. In other words, you are not married to each other but to law. This also means that there is no authority in your marriage. Your marriage may linger on for years as Satan works in your home under the conditions you have provided. Not enough prayer together, reading and sharing Gods word. Not applying the light of scripture and standing on the word of Gods concern about how your household should be run. Giving in to the power of Satan instead of being willing to allow the Holy Spirit to have his way no matter what the cost. "As for me and my house we are going to serve the Lord". (Joshua 24:15) The Holy Spirit does not compromise with anybody. These kinds of relationships will hinder the Church for scripture states if a man know not how to rule his own home, how shall he take care of the Church of God". (I Timothy 3:5) Jesus states "for I have come to set variance against his father, and the daughter against mother, and the daughter-in-law against her mother-in-law. And a man's foes shall be they of his own household. (Matthew 10:35-36) It all comes down to the test of faith in the home. Jesus made the sacrifice to set us free from sin whether in the home or in the world to free us from bondage but we must be willing to accept the power of the Holy Spirit.

PERCEPTION: A DEVICE OF THE MIND

Perception is a device of the mind. And because of the influence that this has on our perceptions, we must also be aware of the spiritual knowledge and condition of our character. Despite our knowledge, the mind can be a field of perceptions good and bad. It will be up to the Spirit to help us make the final decision. But there is always this war of desire, will, and necessary response to any situation. Satan will attack the mind as well as our ability to perceive to honor his purpose. And unless we realize that we are on this spiritual battlefield of the mind we will never know how much we should depend on the Spirit of God for deliverance. Knowledge has a lot to do with how we perceive things. For scripture teaches God say's "my people perish for lack of knowledge". (Hosea 4:6) Since we find ourselves depending on our own knowledge of what we assume we know. That can be a blindness to truth of seeing the whole picture. We need to perceive confirmation of the truth before accepting that perception of that situation. It is only reasonable to perceive in the right way, the truth. Others also expect you to perceive in the right way. But without knowledge it is not possible to make the right decision.

God has provided the man of the house the ability to perceive protectively the issues involving his family in the right direction. He is responsible to God first and then his family in final decisions. It is therefore necessary that he have a special relationship with the Father in heaven as well as a committed example of who is in control. This is why Satan attacks the family and starting with the head of the household. Satan knows if he persuades you from your perspective he can destroy the order and destiny of your family. And likewise, personally effect each individual perception of how to see and manage their lives. Our perception will make all the difference in how we live our lives, make our decisions, and reach our destiny. If we were to turn our perceptions of how we see things over to the Lord we would not have to worry about the right way. For Jesus has said "I am the way the truth and the life no man comes to the Father except by me". (John 14:6, KJV) If the Lord our Father is the head of our house surely, he cannot fail for who He is. He is able to assure us of the right destiny and teach us with the best example of leadership and relationship. (Jude 1:24-25)

We have already turned away from God in obedience, relationships, and principles as Satan has put on our hearts selfishness, and independence. We now live our lives philosophically ignorant of God's righteousness and going about trying to establish our own righteousness. We have not even considered that someone could be deceiving our perceptions and trying to destroy our lives. But until we realize that we are in spiritual warfare and that it's not what you see but how you see it, we will continue in darkness. Perceptions happen every day, all the time, all over the world with everyone. People are even choosing what and how they want to perceive. It could be based on knowledge, hate, love etc. However, man's choice to perceive in this way affects everyone and everything. Since we know that this subject is a greater part of our lives we should not take this for granted.

WHY ARE WE CONCERNED ABOUT THE REALITY OF PERCEPTIONS?

Even though we don't understand the complex relationship that perception has with reality we do know that they both have an effect on our thoughts and influences. Because we live inside a world of perceptions our minds stay consistent with the reality of physical information that is stored in our senses. We cannot separate perception from the reality of our environment but hopefully we can realize that effect that it has on our lives. Like anything else when it comes to moral and discipline expectation perceptual influences needs to be a concern. The answer to such questions as "Why do they act that way? Or "why didn't they handle that differently?" These questions can be answered by stating, they perceived that solution differently. Question is, why? Now we have a problem of what we didn't know.

God has always been concerned about our character even on a personal basis He has commanded us to train up our children in the way they should go in the Lord. (Prov 22:6). What that means is that his perception of how he sees life and his purpose will be made clear; with the proper influences of the word of God. Our character is what's being guided by our perceptions. As the result of this understanding we need to pay close attention to how and why we perceive the way we do in any given situation. Especially in making a decision to react on that situation. If you would take in account seriously the influence of what is right and is wrong when it comes to our belief you will find a strong influence based on our knowledge, what we believe or even what we feel which believe it or not can be drawn away by how we see it. It is always very necessary that we learn how to see the whole picture as it will not only affect us but others around us. Perception is a powerful thing especially in the hand of those who don't realize it. The reality is that we are still responsible for every reaction and response.

Most people don't even see any reason to examine their perceptions or even question their opinions. They simply assume that that's the way it is. But with that kind of attitude the world will never get an understanding of why we do what we do which continues to be a problem. We all don't have to be alike to keep our perceptions in check by trying to see the whole picture. We just need to realize that a lot of bad decisions are being made because of bad perceptions.

Even in scripture Jesus was teaching about what he saw in man (Jn 2:24-25) and (Mt.13-13-15). People's perception depends upon their belief and knowledge as well as their training. The heart of the problem is the person.

People don't realize how important it is to be taught or to get training in everything. It is not just a matter of just being smart but how you see smart. Nobody knows everything so we need to rethink how we see smart to getting familiar with the subject. We are seeing out of blind eyes because we are looking at things the wrong way. For example, in looking at the problem of bullying. The bullying is not the problem but the symptom. Bullying is the result of a greater problem that has not been cured. We hope to look at the whole picture. Most of the time we don't run into "a" problem. It's how you define in your mind what hides behind "a" problem. The fundamental ethics of thinking can remind us how to be in control of our perceptions.

Paul says that a man should examine himself (I Cor 11:28). I'm sure that would include how we think, perceive and react to certain situations out of a loving character as with Christ. How we demonstrate our perception of love spiritually is important. It is our responsibility to live our lives in a perspective way that demonstrates our purpose. There is no excuse for having the wrong perception about anything that renders you to be over powered by the wrong response.

It amazes me that all through the Bible Jesus taught about the perception that men have. The perception of character, perception of Jesus and who he was and the perception of who God is. You would think that Preachers and Bible teachers everywhere would be teaching on this subject realizing the same problem people are having is focusing on our perceptions of Christ. Why is it that we are seeing like we do? Even the effect that perception is having on understanding the difficulties of disciplining themselves and others. It's how we perceive it. Perception is not the answer but Jesus says that it starts with a change of heart. (Prov 23:7, Eccl 8:5) My concern is that more ministers have not approached this reference of concern that needs to be examined. In the process of living the Christian life we know that we are not going to perceive things the way we should all the time. So, we easily introduce the fact that we are sinners and leave that as an excuse instead of examining why we had accepted that perception even though it was not right. Why don't we examine why we had that perception of that issue as well as an issue in our character as a Christian. It could very well affect other issues and perceptions.

It is easy to blame sin for our short coming and sinful nature because we have a sinful perception that we allowed to lead us into a bad situation. Even to say that "the Devil made me do that". But the truth is God holds us responsible to find out how we can avoid that sin and remove from us whatever it was that lead to that perception. (Mk 9:43). We often persuade ourselves because of our perceptions that we didn't have a choice but to respond in that way. We even say that we were not thinking, but we were perceiving? How is that? There is a lot more going on in that perception than we can imagine. Sometimes to understand this we have to consider spirituality. Spiritual perceptibility we can all have, but it requires a change of heart and a relationship with Christ. It is a gift given through the faith that you have in Jesus Christ. It allows you to monitor your life in the words of Jesus Christ and his examples. It will help you to be so familiar with His Spirit that you will know that you are never alone. You will seek in the spirit all of your life and trust in His truth. Your perception will change and so will your heart of understanding. You will see things differently and accurately and the way that the Lord wants you to see yourself and others.

There is a reward according to the word of God for having the right perception. Jesus says he came unto his own and his own received him not. But as many as received him to them gave He power to become the children of God even to them that believed on his name; (John 1:11-12). In other words, there is a right way to perceive and a wrong way to perceive. You have a choice, it does not happen automatically. Never depend on an automatic perception which we do many times. When we learn how to become specific in our insight and understanding then do we become matured. Our source should always be the Spirit of God. Our lives will be so much better if we would use our Spiritual Perceptibility. In every situation, we can and know that God is right there by our side.

CONCLUSION

The whole idea of perception came to me by the Spirit of God while meditating in his word. I realized that many times my perception was not as it should be in understanding of God's messages to me in my studies. Then I realize that it was my perception and thoughts that was getting in the way of the Spirit. I then began to think about how powerful our perceptions effect our lives and that most people don't realize the effect. I began to pray about it while looking further into scripture to see what Jesus said about perception. I was almost surprised but reminded that Jesus addressed the issue all through his teaching by example. Such scriptures as (Matthew 22:16, Mark 8:17, Luke 8:46, John 4:19.

Our perceptions should guide our faith into the right decisions by letting the Spirit take charge of our lives. We are in a spiritual warfare and how we perceive our enemies and our friends is important. "FAITH MEANS WAR" and as we live the faith we have in Jesus Christ we must remember that perception is a tool of the mind ad will make a difference in our decision making in exercising the faith.

BIBLIOGRAPHY OF HELPFUL RESOURCES

Bibles

1. **The New Scofield Reference Bible** C. I. Scofield, D. D., Oxford University Press, Inc, 1967 KJV
2. **The Nelson Study Bible** Thomas Nelson Inc. 1997, Nashville TN NKJV
3. **The Greek New Testament** Biblia-Druck GmbH Stuttgart, West Germany, Third Edition 1983
4. **The NIV Thematic Reference Bible**, Zondervan Publishing House, 1984 International Bible Society

5. <u>The Living Bible</u>, Tyndale House Publishers, Inc, Wheaton, Illinois, 1971
6. <u>NASB Study Bible,</u> Zondervan 1995, New American Standard Bible

<u>Biblical Resource Tool</u>

1. Dictionary of Paul and His Letters, Intervarsity Press, 1993
2. Dictionary of Biblical Imagery IVP Academic, Inter Varsity Press, 1998
3. Vine's Expository Dictionary of New Testament Words, Barbour and Company, Inc. 1985

SCRIPTURE
REFERENCES

Ephesians 6:10-12

Genesis 1:28

Genesis 2:17

Genesis 3: 15-16

II Timothy 3:12

Ephesians 6:16

II Timothy 2:4

Revelation 2:10

Ephesians 6:13

Ephesians 2:2

Revelation 12:17

II Corinthians 10:4-6

Hebrew 4:12

Jude 3

Jude 6

Joshua 24:15

I Kings 18:22

I Kings 19:1

Daniel 10:21

Daniel 10:13

Ephesians 6:11

Acts 13:6

Acts 13:12

John 5:4

Daniel 11:45

II Corinthians 10:4

Revelation 12:12

John 13:33

James 1:1-2

II Corinthians 8:2

Zechariah 4:6

Hebrew 5:8

Romans 8:28

Matthew 28:20

Romans 7:22-24

Luke 9:62

II Timothy 2:3-4

Hebrew 1:1

Hebrew 11-6

Genesis 4:1-8-8, 14

Genesis 2:16-17

Genesis 3:5-7:22

Matthew 22:21

Genesis 6:3

Deuteronomy 13:6-7

Deuteronomy 13:8-13

II Timothy 3:12

Micah 7:5-6

James 4:1-3

I Peter 1:7

I Corinthians 3:13

II Timothy 3:15

I Timothy 6:12

I Timothy 1:18

Acts 1:18

Matthew 9:8

Matthew 28:18

John 6:63

Matthew 6:33

John 12:32

Nehemiah 4:6

I Thessalonians 5:23

Romans 7:15-24

I Peter 1:13

I Peter 1:10-14

Romans 12:2

Philippians 2:5

Romans 12:1-2

Ephesians 5:9-12

Romans 7:24-25

Judges 5:8

Proverb 16:25

John 17:11

Romans 13:8

II Corinthians 6:14

I Corinthians 7:12-16

I Corinthians 15:33

Ps 5:5

II Corinthians 13:5

Matthew 6:24

Luke 17:16

Matthew 16:24

Luke 14:28

Ecclesiastes 8:8

Hosea 4:6

Jude 1:24-25

Proverb 33:6

John 2:24-25

Matthew 13:13-15

I Corinthians 11:28

Proverb 23:7

Ecclesiastes 8:5

Mark 9:43

John 1:11-12

ABOUT THE AUTHOR

Larry E Adams earned his BS, MS, Ph. D from Lael College & Graduate School and has received certifications in advanced Biblical studies from Missouri Baptist College. He is a Board Certified Biblical Counselor and has been a Bible teacher for forty years at the St. Timothy M. B. Church in St. Louis, Missouri, where he and his wife, Julia continue to serve the Lord faithfully.